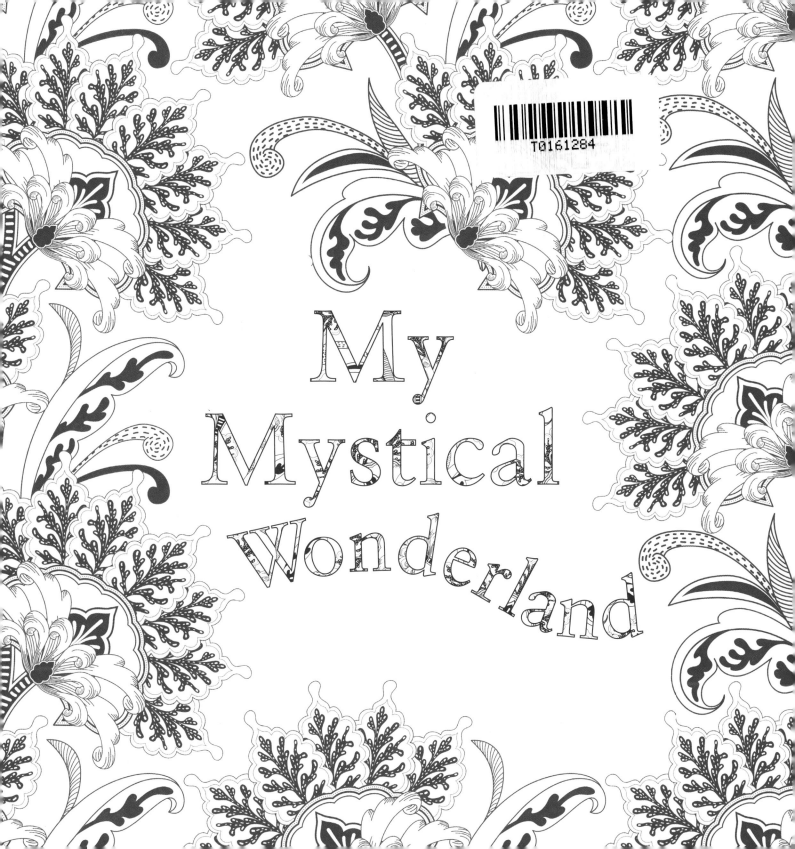

My Mystical Wonderland

My Mystical Wonderland

Art Therapy Colouring Book For Creative Minds

Illustrated by
Eglantine de la Fontaine
& Various Artists

Plexus, London

Introducing *My Mystical Wonderland*, a book for doodling and dreaming in every shade of the rainbow

Wherever you're from and whatever the colour of your dreams, *My Mystical Wonderland* offers a uniquely creative escape from the stresses and strains of everyday life.

Allow yourself to be transported over the hills and faraway . . . to a tangled forest filled with flighty fairytale creatures – glimpsed only in dreams and the pages of your favourite story books. Stretching to the very limits of your imagination and beyond, all that's truly missing from this enchanted woodland is a splash of rainbow light.

Can you colour between the lines to bring this intricate inky world to life? Gather together a set of fine felt-tips or coloured pencils (the latter will help you create subtle shades rather than bright primary blocks) and prepare to be delighted by the results.

And that's not all. Peppered with enticing blank spaces and empty outlines, more confident artists will relish the opportunity to fill in detailed doodles of their own . . . or not. If it's more relaxing for you to stick within the lines, then this is perfectly acceptable too. Perhaps there are some corners of the woodland that you prefer to leave untouched in shades of black and white? Within *My Mystical Wonderland*, there are no rules, limits or requirements . . . simply the pleasure of creating beautiful pictures that you'll want to keep forever. So, relax, enjoy – and prepare to lose yourself in a world of silver bells, cockleshells and pretty ferns all in a row.

Eglantine

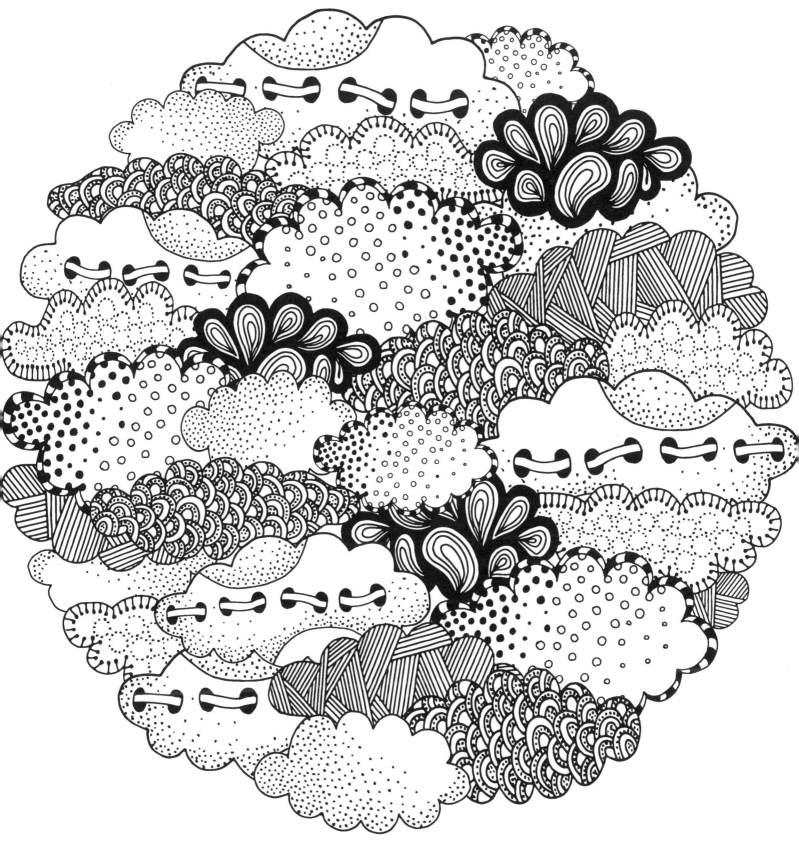

Fine, feathery touches are all you'll need to complete this magic circle – so make a wish and fill them in.

Sketch more swirly tendrils to keep these faraway trees rooted firmly to the ground.

Colour the feathers of this preening peacock till they shine like jewels – and he'll never be lonesome again.

These enchanted vines are growing like wild fire! Sketch more berries and blooms if you think you can keep up.

Fill this little gecko's back with intricate inky markings so he fits in with the rest of the family.

This fiery dragon's been robbed by an impertinent prince! Can you sketch him a brand-new hoard to keep him happy?

Decorate these butterfly wings with fine lacy detail – and let your imagination take flight!

Harvest time is here! So imagine the most fanciful fruit that you can. Once you've dreamed it; draw it.

Use this outline to create a mesmerising masque . . . fit for a princess at a ball.

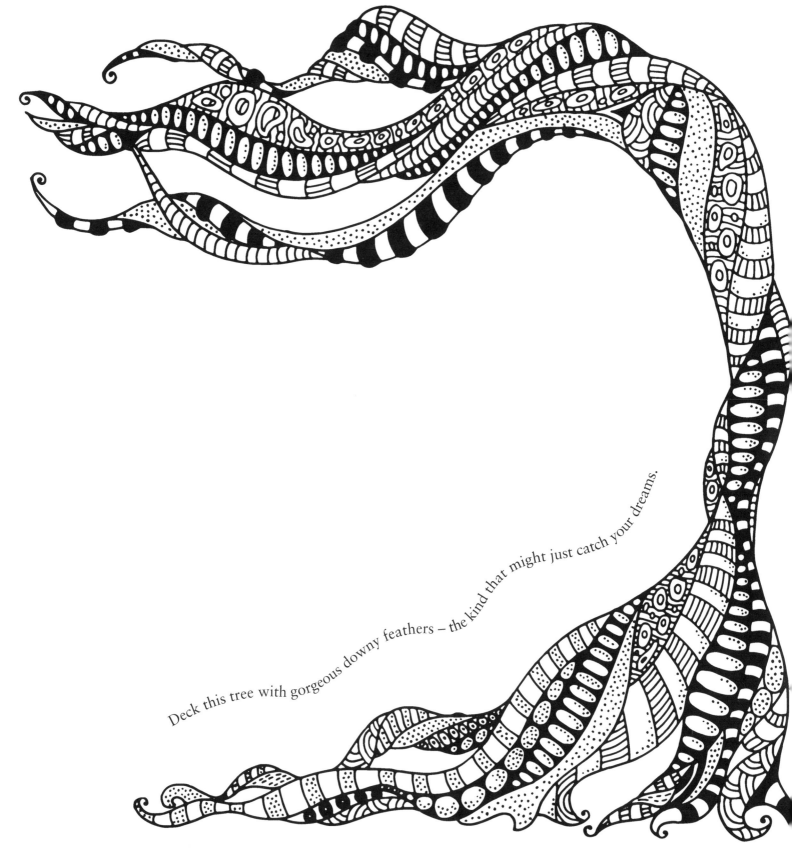

Deck this tree with gorgeous downy feathers – the kind that might just catch your dreams.

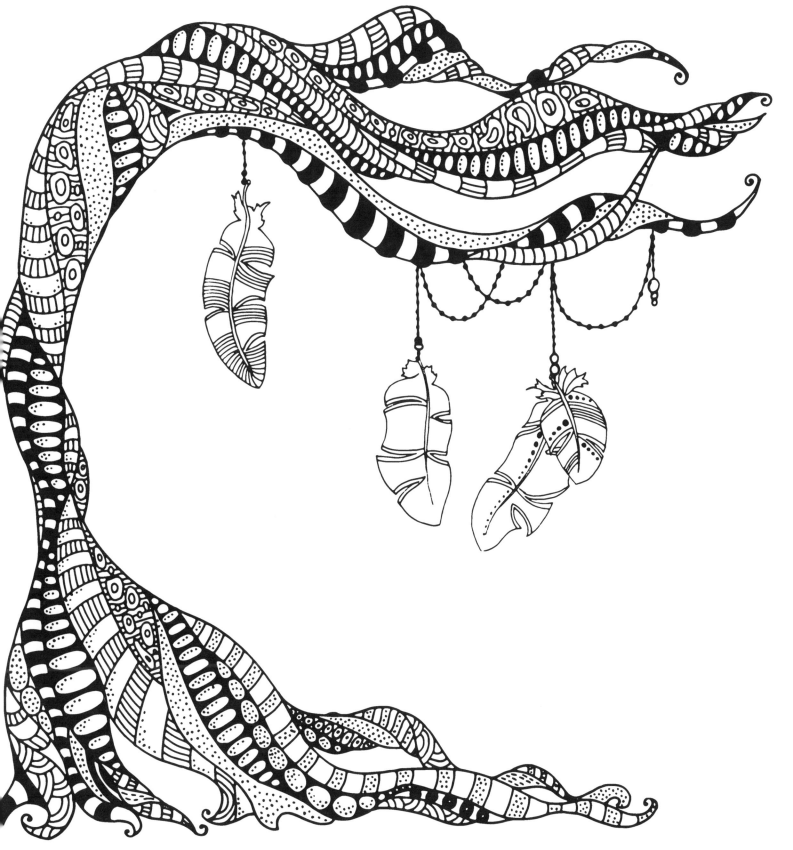

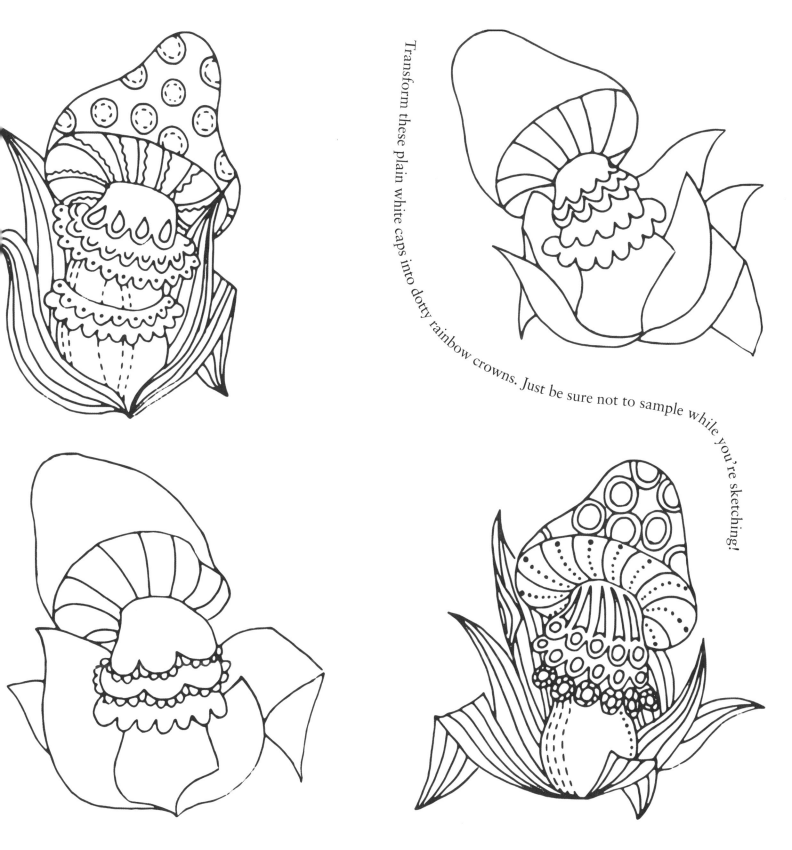

Transform these plain white caps into dotty rainbow crowns. Just be sure not to sample while you're sketching!

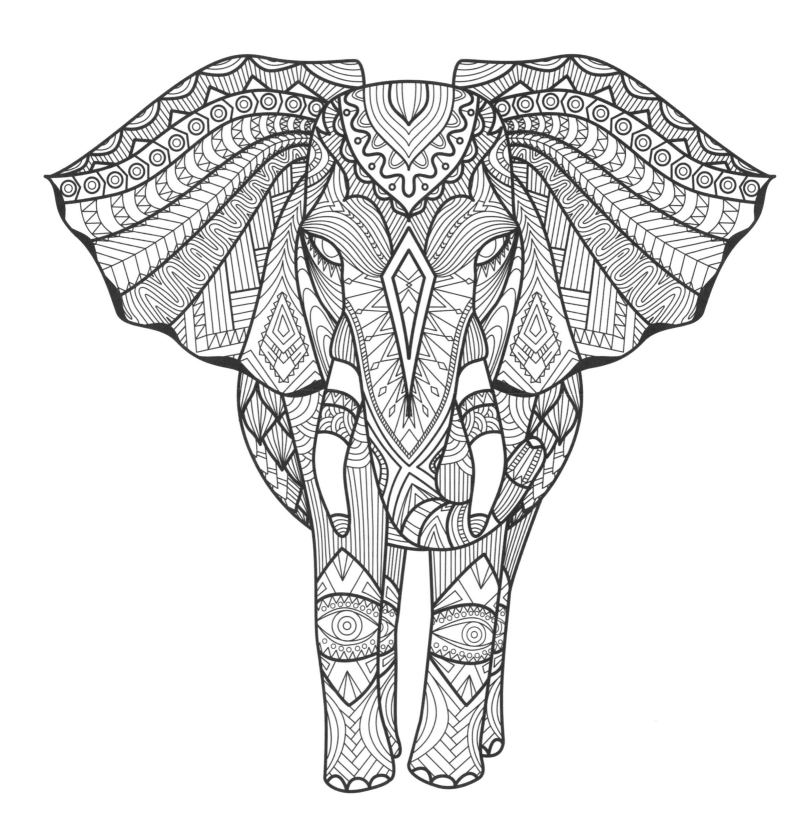

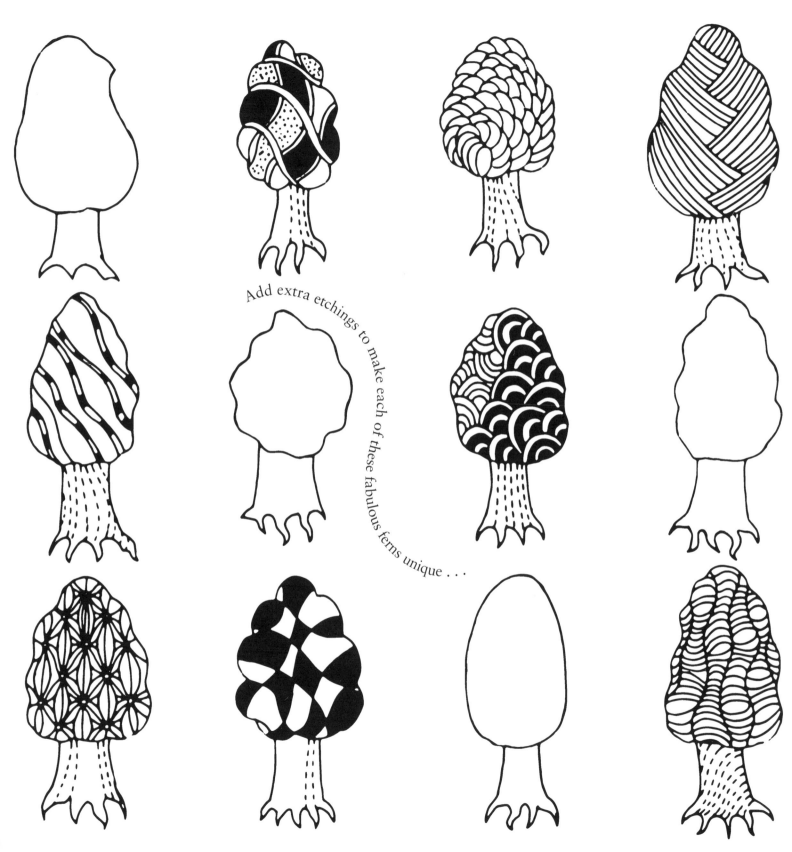

Add extra etchings to make each of these fabulous ferns unique . . .

First published in 2016 by Plexus Publishing Limited
Copyright © 2016 by Plexus Publishing Limited
Published by Plexus Publishing Limited
The Studio, Hillgate Place,
18-20 Balham Hill, London SW12 9ER
www.plexusbooks.com

British Library Cataloguing in Publication Data
A catalogue record for this book is available
from the British Library

ISBN-13: 978-0-85965-543-9

Illustrations by Eglantine de la Fontaine & various artists
Cover design by Coco Balderrama
Book design by Coco Balderrama
Printed in Great Britain by Bell & Bain Ltd, Glasgow

Thanks to Laura Coulman.
With additional material adapted from www.shutterstock.com

Previous title: My Magical Oasis